# How To Speak Arabic in Jordan

## Easy Arabic Phrasebook With Travel Tips

ESZTER PAPAI

# DEDICATION

To my kids and my husband, who keep teaching me new Arabic words every day.

# CONTENTS

# ACKNOWLEDGMENTS

I was given considerable help by many Jordanian people in writing and formatting this book. Thank you all.

Various online Arabic language resources were also used to double-check everything.
Their detailed references are listed in Chapter 20.

# 1 IS THIS BOOK FOR YOU?

**This book is for you if ...**

... you don't have much time to learn to read and write in Arabic but ...

... you want to be able to have simple conversations with local people in everyday situations and ...

... you want to understand why people in Jordan do or say certain things.

This phrasebook is a brief introduction of the Arabic language spoken in Jordan, accompanied by some "travel guide-ish" information:

- **cultural notes** and **interesting facts** that will deepen your understanding of the country and its people.

- also includes lots of **useful tips** and even live **links to resources** that will save you time when planning out your trip.

**However, this book is NOT for you if ....**

... your main goal with learning Arabic is to understand Arab media, science or poetry.

... your main goal is to learn to read and write in Arabic.

... your main goal with learning Arabic is to read the Holy Koran.

In these cases you must study Standard Arabic (al-fuSHa) that is being taught at Western universities and language courses.

See Arabic language resources at the end of this book.

*SIDENOTE:*

*Standard Arabic is used in the media (TV, radio, newspapers and magazines), literature and formal writing in general, and official occasions.*

*However, Arabs don't speak Standard Arabic in their daily lives. They grow up speaking their own dialects and only start to learn fuSHa in school. Later, after finishing their education, many Arabs lose a great deal of their active knowledge of fuSHa, particularly the details of grammar rules.*

The main dialects of colloquial Arabic language are:

1. **Maghrebi** - spoken in Northern African countries like Algeria, Morocco, and Tunisia. This dialect is the farthest from Standard Arabic with many loan words from French and it's difficult to understand even for other Arabs.

2. **Egyptian** - spoken in Egypt. This is the most widely understood dialect, thanks to the huge Egyptian music, TV, and film industry that is very popular all around the Arab world.

3. **Levantine** - spoken in Lebanon, Syria, Palestine, and **Jordan**.

4. **Gulf** or **Khaliiji** - spoken in the Gulf countries.

In each of these regions are various local sub-dialects (for example, in Jordan there're the urban Ammani, Keraki, Tafileh, etc. and rural Bedouin sub-dialects) but they have enough in common to be classified in one category, and people from different parts of the same region will have no trouble understanding each other.

## About this book

This book is divided into chapters. Each chapter is focusing in one subject and presenting the vocabulary in a table format:

- **English Meaning** in the middle column with the

- **Arabic Script** in the right column and the

- **Pronunciation Guide** with transliterations in the left column.

As there is no one single method of transliteration of Arabic script into English, to keep things as simple as possible, this book uses the Roman alphabet only.

Read the words as an English speaker would pronounce them.

I also included lots of white space where you can add your own notes.

Feel free to jot down new words you learn during your travels by interacting with native speakers.

Notes:

*..... The "Notes" sections are for you to write down your own findings, ideas, experiences or memories throughout the entire book .....*

# 2 GREETINGS & INTRODUCTIONS

Greetings are a sign of respect in every culture. If get the basics right, even if your pronunciation is not perfect, people will really appreciate your efforts.

As a general rule, men shake hands and kiss cheeks only with men and women only with women.

In Islamic cultures a woman can only be touched by her very close male relatives: father, son, brother, husband, grandfather or uncle.

So if you are a man, don't try to shake hands with a local woman, unless she offers it first.

## COMMON GREETINGS

You can't go wrong by using the following common greetings.  You can say it to anybody, anytime, anywhere:

| Pronunciation | English meaning | Arabic script |
|---|---|---|
| assalamu 'alaikum | Peace be upon you | السلام عليكم |
| (wa) 'alaikum assalam | (and) Peace be upon you | ( و) عليكم السلام |

| Pronunciation | English meaning | Arabic script |
|---|---|---|
| marHaba | Hello | مرحبا |
| ahlain / hala | Hello (reply) | أهلين/ هلا |

| Pronunciation | English meaning | Arabic script |
|---|---|---|
| Salaam | Peace | سلام |

| Pronunciation | English meaning | Arabic script |
|---|---|---|
| ahlan wa sahlan | Welcome | أهلا و سهلا |
| ahlan beek | Hello (reply to a man) | أهلا بيك |
| ahlan beeki | Hello (reply to a woman) | أهلا بيكي |

| Pronunciation | English meaning | Arabic script |
|---|---|---|
| Ma' asslamah | Good bye | مع السلامة |
| Ma' asslamah | Good bye | مع السلامة |

## GREETINGS ACCORDING TO TIME OF THE DAY

During the day, between "morning" and "evening", just simply use the Common Greetings above.

Here are the special phrases for morning and evening:

| Pronunciation | English meaning | Arabic script |
|---|---|---|
| SabaH elKhair | Good morning | صباح الخير |
| SabaH ennoor | Good morning (reply) | صباح النور |
| Pronunciation | English meaning | Arabic script |
| Masaa elKhair | Good evening | مساء الخير |
| Masaa ennoor | Good evening (reply) | مساء النور |
| Pronunciation | English meaning | Arabic script |
| TuSbaaH elKhair | Good night | تصبح على خير |
| O enta bkher | Good night (reply) | وانته بخير |

Notes:

# 3 USEFUL PHRASES

These common expressions are used in almost every conversation, any situation.

## Yellah! – Let's get started!

*"Yellah!"* is probably the most often used word in Arabic.

You can use it as a question:

*"Yellah?"* - meaning: *"Shall we?"* go/do/start whatever we were about to do or start.

The answer is, of course: *"Yellah!"* - *"Let's!"*

| Pronunciation | English meaning | Arabic script |
|---|---|---|
| Aywa / na'am | Yes | أيوا/ نعم |
| la | No | لا |
| shukran | Thank you | شكراً |
| afwan | You are welcome | عفواً |
| mumken | It is possible / Is it possible? | ممكن |
| TfaDDal (to a man) / tfaDDalii (to a woman) | Please (be my guest) | تفضل / تفضلي |
| aassef | Sorry | آسف |
| mish mushkelah! | No problem | مش مشكلة |

Notes:

| Pronunciation | English meaning | Arabic script |
|---|---|---|
| yellah | Come on! Let's go! | يللا |
| Mashii / tayyeb | OK / All right | ماشي / طيّب |
| 'aadii | Normal (nothing special) | عادي |
| Estanna shwai | Please wait a bit | استنى شوي |
| Dageega bas | Just a minute! | دقيقة بس |
| Wen el hammam | Where is the toilet? | وين الحم |

Notes:

# 4 SMALL TALK

**How are you?**

People in Jordan usually respond to "*How are you?*"

with "A*l-Hamdulillah.*" which means "Thank the God".

They say it even if they are not feeling well. It's a religious concept that you has to be grateful to God in any circumstances.

When two Jordanians meet they place great importance on proper greetings and lengthy inquiries into each other's health, families etc.

You can sometimes overhear people taking a phone call and spending the next two minutes with such formalities before even finding out who is calling!

This is quite the opposite of the Western concept of
"Time is money".

| Pronunciation | English meaning | Arabic script |
|---|---|---|
| Kaif Halak? (to a man) | How are you? | ( كيف حالَك؟ ) للرجل |
| (to a woman) | How are you? | ( كيف حالِك؟ ) للأنثى |
| Ana kwayes (man) / Ana kwaysa (woman) alHamdulillah | Fine, Thank the God. | أنا كويس ( للرجل ) / أنا كويسة ( للأنثى ) الحمدلله |
| **Pronunciation** | **English meaning** | **Arabic script** |
| *Shu ismak* | | شو اسمك؟ |
| Ismi John. | My name is John. | إسمي جون |
| **Pronunciation** | **English meaning** | **Arabic script** |
| Min wen enta? | Where are you from? | من وين انته ؟ |
| Ana min ... | I'm from ... | أنا من ... |

## Where do you come from?

For sure, everyone you are talking to will want to know where you are coming from.

The table below is a non-complete list of the countries where most of the tourists arrive from., hopefully you can find yours too.

| Pronunciation | English meaning | Arabic script |
| --- | --- | --- |
| Amrekia | America (the USA) | أمريكيا |
| Kanada | Canada | كندا |
| Orobba | Europe | أوروبا |
| Engiltra | England | إنجلترا |
| Bretania | Britain | بريطانيا |
| Almania | Germany | ألمانيا |
| Faransa | France | فرنسا |
| Holanda | Holland | هولندا |
| Baljekia | Begium | بلجيكيا |
| Etalia | Italy | إيطاليا |

| Pronunciation | English meaning | Arabic script |
|---|---|---|
| Espania | Spain | إسبانيا |
| El barazil | Brazil | البرازيل |
| El arjantin | Argentina | الأرجنتين |
| El namsa | Austria | النمسا |
| Hongaria | Hungary | هونغاريا |
| Bolanda | Poland | بولندا |
| Roosia | Russia | روسيا |
| Elseen | China | الصين |
| El hind | India | الهند |
| El yaban | Japan | اليابان |
| Ostralia | Australia | أستراليا |
| Neoozlanda | New Zealand | نيوزلندا |

How is YOUR country called in Arabic?

Notes:

# 5 COMMUNICATION DIFFICULTIES

When you don't quite understand what people are telling you, ask them to repeat it, say it slowly or write down the information you need - like an address or timetable, for example.

While having problems making yourself understood can be frustrating, try to consider these situations as chances to improve your Arabic: to learn new words and phrases.

Local people will be happy to help you.

| Pronunciation | English meaning | Arabic script |
|---|---|---|
| Ma bahki arabi | I don't speak Arabic | ما بحكي عربي |
| Bahki shwai arabi | I speak a little Arabic | بحكي شوي عربي |
| Fhimit | I understand | فهمت |
| Ma fhimit | I don't understand | ما فهمت |
| Law samaht t'eed kalamak | Please say it again | لو سمحت تعيد كلامك |
| La samaht ihki abta' shwai | Please speak slowly | لو سمحت احكي أبطئ شوي |
| Law samaht iktobli yaha | Write it down please | لو سمحت اكتبلي ياها |
| Sho ma'naha? | What does it mean? | شو معناها؟ |
| shu isim haada bil Arabi? | What is it called in Arabic? | شو اسم هادا بالعربي |
| kiif bitquul...... bil Arabi? | How do you say ... in Arabic? | كيف بتقول ... بالعربي |

Notes:

# 6 QUESTION WORDS

These few basic question words are very useful to know.

By combining them with simple nouns (names of things, for example) you will be able to find out just about anything you want.

| Pronunciation | English meaning | Arabic script |
|---|---|---|
| Shuu | What | شو |
| Miin | Who | مين |
| aimta / mata | When | متى / ايمتى |
| Kaif | How | آيف |
| Wain | Where | وين |
| Gaddaish | How much / How many | قديش |
| Ayy | Which | أيّ |
| Leesh | Why | ليش |

Notes:

Notes:

# 7 NUMBERS

After Greetings and *"Thank you"*, numbers are probably the most important for travelers to learn as you encounter them in various situations:

- shopping and bargaining

- telling the time

- opening hours

- timetables etc.

These number-related subjects are listed in this chapter as sub-chapters.

# ORDINARY NUMBERS

| Pronunciation | English meaning | Arabic script |
|:---:|:---:|:---:|
| Siffer | 0 - Zero | صف |
| waHad | 1 - One | واحد |
| Ethnain | 2 – Two | اثنين |
| Thalatha | 3 - Three | ثلاثة |
| arba'a | 4 - Four | اربعة |
| Khamsa | 5 - Five | خمسة |
| Sitta | 6 - Six | ستة |
| saba'a | 7 - Seven | سبعة |
| Thamania | 8 - Eight | ثمانية |
| tesa'a | 9 - Nine | تسعة |
| 'ashara | 10 - Ten | عشرة |

| Pronunciation | English meaning | Arabic script |
|---|---|---|
| Ehdash | 11 - Eleven | احداش |
| Ethna'sh | 12 - Twelve | اثناعش |
| Thalathta'sh | 13 - Thirteen | ثلثتاعش |
| Arba'tash | 14 - Fourteen | أربعتاش |
| Khamesta'sh | 15 - Fifteen | خمستاش |
| Sitta'sh | 16 - Sixteen | ستاش |
| Saba'tash | 17 - Seventeen | سبعتاش |
| Thamanta'sh | 18 - Eighteen | ثمنتاش |
| Tes'tash | 19 - Nineteen | تسعتاش |
| Eshreen | 20 - Twenty | عشرين |
| Wahad o eshreen | 21 – One and Twenty | واحد وعشرين |
| Ethneen o eshreen | 22 – Two and Twenty | اثنين وعشرين |

| Pronunciation | English meaning | Arabic script |
|---|---|---|
| Thalatheen | 30 - Thirty | ثلاثين |
| Arba'een | 40 - Fourty | أربعين |
| Khamseen | 50 - Fifty | خمسين |
| Sitteen | 60 - Sixty | ستين |
| Sab'een | 70 - Seventy | سبعين |
| Thamaneen | 80 - Eighty | ثمانين |
| Tes'een | 90 - Ninety | تسعين |
| Meieh | 100 – Hundred | مية |
| Metain | 200 – Two hundred | ميتين |
| Thathmieh | 300 – Three hundred | ثلاثمية |
| Alf | 1,000 - Thousand | ألف |
| Aflen | 2,000 – Two thousand | ألفين |

| Pronunciation | English meaning | Arabic script |
|---|---|---|
| Thalath alaf | 3,000 – Three thousand | ثلاث آلاف |
| Malioon | 1,000,000 - One million | مليون |

## TELLING THE TIME

There are several ways to refer to time. For example, when arranging a meeting we can talk about an exact point in time.

| Pronunciation | English meaning | Arabic script |
|---|---|---|
| Kam el sa'a | What's the time? | كم الساعة؟ |
| El sa'a 5 | It's 5 o'clock | الساعة 5 |
| Sa'a | hour | ساعة |
| Dageega | minute | دقيقة |
| Nos sa'a | Half an hour | نص ساعة |
| Robe' sa'a | Quarter of an hour | ربع ساعة |
| 5:30 | 5:30h | **5:30** |
| Khamseh o nos | Half past five | خمسة ونص |
| 6:15 | 6:15h | **6:15** |
| Sitteh o robe' | Quarter past six | ستة وربع |
| Pronunciation | English meaning | Arabic script |
| 6:45 | 6.45h | **6:45** |
| Sab'a illa robe' | Quarter to 7 | سبعة الا ربع |

| Pronunciation | English meaning | Arabic script |
|---|---|---|
| Sab'a illa 15 dageega | 15 minutes to 7 | سبعة الا 15 دقيقة |
| 7:05 | 7:05h | 7:05 |
| 6:55 = sab'a ( 7 ) illa 5 dagayeg | 6:55h = 5 (min) to 7 (o'clock) | 6:55 = ( 7 ) سبعة إلا 5 دقايق |
| Pronunciation | English meaning | Arabic script |
| El sa'a sab'a el sobeh | 7 o'clock in the morning | الساعة سبعة الصبح |
| El sa'a sab'a billel | 7 o'clock in the night | الساعة سبعة بالليل |

We can also refer to certain parts of a day:

| Pronunciation | English meaning | Arabic script |
|---|---|---|
| Shoroq el shams | sunrise | شروق الشمس |
| Sabahan | morning | الصبح |
| Dohr | noon | الظهر |

| Ba'd el dohr ( asir ) | afternoon | ( بعد الظهر ( العصر |
|---|---|---|
| Al maghrib | sunset | غروب الشمس ( المغرب ) ) |
| El masa | evening | المسا |
| Fil lel | night | في الليل |

Being predominantly Muslim country, the five prayer times also gives a certain frame of life for people in Jordan.

You can often hear them saying that they will do something *"after the sunset prayer"* or *"after the afternoon prayer"*.

On the next page you can find the names of the five daily prayers.

Their exact time is determined by the sun's situation on the sky so every day they are a couple of minutes earlier or later than the day before.

The Sunset Prayer is especially important during the month of **Ramadan**, as it marks the end of the daily fast.

If you want to know when exactly the prayer times are during your visit to Jordan, you can check it out on http://islamicfinder.org/

| Pronunciation | English meaning | Arabic script |
|---|---|---|
| Salat el Fajr | Break of the dawn prayer | صلاة الفجر |
| Salat el dohr | Noon prayer | صلاة الظهر |
| Salat el asr | Afternoon prayer | صلاة العصر |
| Salat el maghrib | Sunset prayer | صلاة المغرب |
| Salat el esha' | Night prayer | صلاة العشاء |

Notes:

# TELLING YOUR AGE

| Pronunciation | English meaning | Arabic script |
| --- | --- | --- |
| Kam omrak? | How old are you? | كم عمرك؟ |
| Omri 35 saneh | I'm 35 (years old) | عمري 35 سنة |

Notes:

## MONEY & PRICES

Jordan's official currency is the Dinar. In the everyday language it is also called "laira".

1 "dinar" equals 100 "gersh" or "piaster".

The Jordanian Dinar (JOD or JD) is pegged to the USD. The exchange rate is

1 JOD = 1.4 USD

1 USD = 0.7 JOD

| Pronunciation | English meaning | Arabic script |
|---|---|---|
| Masari (floos) | money | (مصاري)فلوس |
| Dinar | dinar | دينار |
| Qirsh | piaster | قرش |
| Fills | Fils, qirsh | فلس |
| Kam se'erha | How much is it? | كم سعرها؟ |
| Se'erha dinar 1 | It's 1 dinar. | سعرها 1 دينار |
| Se'erha dinaren | It's 2 dinars. | سعرها دينارين |

| Pronunciation | English meaning | Arabic script |
|---|---|---|
| Se'erha 5 qroosh | It's 5 qirsh | سعرها 5 قروش |
| 25 qirsh = 0.25 dinar ( robe' dinar) | It's 25 piasters = 0.25 dinar | قرش = 0.25 25 ( دينار ( ربع دينار |
| Robe' dinar | It's quarter dinar. | ربع دينار |
| Nos dinar | It's half dinar. | نص دينار |
| 4 dananeer o nos | It's 4.50 (four and a half( | دنانير ونص 4 |

Notes:

## MEASUREMENTS

Jordan uses the metric system but some products (especially imported ones) indicate the imperial equivalent too on their labels.

So when you are shopping for fruits, vegetables, meat or fish, ask for a kilo, half kilo etc.

### Dunum

There is one special unit for land area measurement: **dunum**. Originally it was used in the Ottoman Empire which Jordan was once part of.

You don't really need it, unless you are buying or renting land, of course.

1 metric dunum equals 1,000 sqm.

| Pronunciation | English meaning | Arabic script |
|---|---|---|
| Ghram | Gramm, g | غرام ، غ |
| Keloghram | Kilogramm, kg | كيلوغرام، كغم |
| Meter | Meter, m | متر ، م |
| Santemeter | Centimeter, cm | سنتميتر، سم |
| Millemeter | Millimeter, mm | مللميتر، مم |
| Kelometer | Kilometer, km | كيلومتر، كم |
| Donom | Dunum | دونوم |
| Leter | Liter, l | ليتر، ل |
| Milleltr | Milliliter, ml | مللیلتر، مل |
| Meter morabba' | Square meter, sqm | متر مربع، م 2 |
| Meter moka'ab | Cubic meter, cu m | متر مكعب، م 3 |
| Darajeh mi'awiyeh | Degrees Celsius | درجة مئوية |

# 8 CALENDAR

In Jordan the week starts on Sunday and the weekend is Friday and Saturday.

Shops and restaurants are open every day, only on Friday they open later: after the mid-day prayer.

| Pronunciation | English meaning | Arabic script |
|---|---|---|
| Yom | day | يوم |
| Osbo' | week | اسبوع |
| Shahar | month | شهر |
| Saneh | year | سنة |
| A'qd | decade | عقد |
| Qarn | century | قرن |
| Alfiyeh | millennia | ألفية |

## DAYS OF THE WEEK

Do you need to book a ticket or do you want to go somewhere that is only open on certain days of the week?

Maybe someone would like to arrange a meeting with you, or you need to explain when a regular event occurs.

Once you know these seven Arabic words, you'll be able to use them in countless ways.

| Pronunciation | English meaning | Arabic script |
|:---:|:---:|:---:|
| Ahad | Sunday | الأحد |
| Ithnen | Monday | الإثنين |
| Thalatha | Tuesday | الثلاثا |
| Arbi'a | Wednesday | الأربعا |
| Khamees | Thursday | الخميس |
| Jom'a | Friday | الجمعة |
| Sabt | Saturday | السبت |

## NAMES OF THE MONTHS

The months are useful to know also whether you wan to tell when your birthday is or when you are planning to go somewhere.

| Pronunciation | English meaning | Arabic script |
|---|---|---|
| Kanoon el thani | January | كانون الثاني |
| Shobat | February | شباط |
| Adhar | March | آذار |
| Nesan | April | نيسان |
| Ayyar | May | أيار |
| hozairan | June | حزيران |
| Tammooz | July | تموز |
| Aab | August | آب |
| A'ilool | September | أيلول |
| Tishreen el awwal | October | تشرين الأول |

| Pronunciation | English meaning | Arabic script |
|---|---|---|
| Tishreen el thani | November | تشرين الثاني |
| Kanoon el awwal | December | كانون الأول |

Notes:

# 9  WEATHER & SEASONS

Whether you're making travel plans or just chatting with locals, words about weather and the seasons are handy to know.

What's a good time of year to visit?

Is it nicer to travel in autumn or spring?

How are the seasons in Jordan compared to the seasons in your country?


For more info about the weather in Jordan and the best time to visit: http://www.your-guide-to-aqaba-jordan.com/weather-in-jordan.html

## NAMES OF THE 4 SEASONS

| Pronunciation | English meaning | Arabic script |
|:---:|:---:|:---:|
| Rabee' | Spring | ربيع |
| Sayf | Summer | صيف |
| khareef | Autumn, Fall | خريف |
| Shita | Winter | شتاء |

Notes:

# WEATHER-RELATED WORDS & EXPRESSIONS

| Pronunciation | English meaning | Arabic script |
|---|---|---|
| Shoroq el shams | sunshine | شروق الشمس |
| Jaw moshmis | Sunny weather | جو مشمس |
| El jaw hami | It's very hot | الجو حامي |
| El sama mghaymeh | Cloudy sky | السما مغيمة |
| matar | Rain | مطر |
| Rah tishte el yom? | Will it rain today? | راح تشتي اليوم؟ |
| Asef | Windy | عاصف |
| El dinya bard | It's cold | الدنيا برد |
| Thalj | snow | ثلج |
| Asifeh thaljiyeh | blizzard | عاصفة ثلجية |
| Asifeh ramliyeh | sandstorm | عاصفة رملية |

**Notes:**

# 10 COLORS

Knowing the names of colors can be useful when you are shopping for clothes or souvenirs, for example.

The table on the next page includes the basic colors.

Feel free to ask the local Bedoiuns how they describe the million shades of red in Wadi Rum or Petra!

| Pronunciation | English meaning | Arabic script |
|---|---|---|
| *aswad* | black | اسود |
| *abyaD* | white | ابيض |
| *ramaadi* | grey | رمادي |
| *aHmar* | red | احمر |
| *azraq* | blue | ازرق |
| *aSfar* | yellow | اصفر |
| *akhDar* | green | اخضر |
| *burtuqaali* | orange | برتقالي |
| Banafsaji | purple | بنفسجي |
| Buuni | brown | بني |

Notes:

Notes:

# 11 FOOD & MEALS

If you are invited to someone's home for lunch or dinner, don't be surprised if the food is served on the carpet.

Eating on the floor is quite usual in Jordan, when everyone gathers around a large round plate of rice and meat.

Sometimes men and women and served in two separate rooms.

For men, it is acceptable to sit the Indian style or with your legs underneath you, but women should sit with their legs pulled in to one side.

Pointing the soles of your feet at anyone is considered rude so don't do it.

The eating starts with saying "Bismillah" (in the name of God) aloud.

Always use your right hand when eating and drinking.

Say "al-Hamdullillah" (Thank the God) when you finish you meal.

## MAIN MEALS

Breakfast usually consists of bread, white cheese, olives, eggs, oil and thyme, tomatoes and sometimes Falafel, Hummus or Fuul on Fridays.

Lunch is considered the main meal in Jordan and it's usually served in the afternoon when kids get home from school.

After the main dish sweet tea (shai) is served and sometimes sweets, cakes or fruit.

Dinner is usually served late at night. It consists of the same elements as in breakfast.

The round Arabic bread (khubuz) is served with each meal.

When invited, it is not polite to leave immediately after having a meal. Your hosts would never ask

you to leave so if you feel that it is time to go, you must come up with a good excuse.

Even then, your hosts will probably try to convince you to stay a bit more.

## JORDAN'S NATIONAL DISH

The traditional dish in Jordan is "Mansaf" which consists of rice, cooked yoghurt and either chicken or meat.

It is usually served at big celebrations like weddings as a way of showing great respect for guests.

Other popular dishes in Jordan – check the ones that you had tried!

Maglouba / Shwarma / Kebab / Shistaouk / Koftah / Kabseh / Falafel / Molokhia /......

Notes:

## RAMADAN

During the month of Ramadan the dinner, served right after the sunset, becomes the main meal. It is actually called "*breakfast*" (iftar)

## MEALS

| Pronunciation | English meaning | Arabic script |
|---|---|---|
| Ftoor | Breakfast | فطور |
| Ghada | Lunch | غدا |
| 'asha | Dinner | عشا |
| Ftoor ba'd el syam | Breakfast after the fast | فطور بعد الصيام |
| Syam | Fasting | صيام |

Notes:

## BASIC FOOD ITEMS

| Pronunciation | English meaning | Arabic script |
|---|---|---|
| Wajbeh | Food, meal | وجبة |
| Khobez | bread | خبز |
| Zibdeh | butter | زبدة |
| Jibneh | cheese | جبنة |
| Laban | yoghurt | لبن |
| Zaitoon | olives | زيتون |
| Baid | eggs | بيض |
| Baid masloog | Hard boiled eggs | بيض مسلوق |
| Baid magli | Scrambled eggs | بيض مقلي |
| 'ijjeh | omlet | عجة |
| Zait zaitoon | Olive oil | زيت زيتون |
| Za'tar | thyme | زعتر |
| 'Asal | honey | عسل |

| Pronunciation | English meaning | Arabic script |
|---|---|---|
| Mrabba | jam | مربى |

Notes:

## MEAT, FISH & SEAFOOD

| Pronunciation | English meaning | Arabic script |
|---|---|---|
| Lahmeh | meat | لحمة |
| Lahmet kharoof | lamb | لحمة خروف |
| Lahamet baqar | beef | لحمة بقر |
| Lahmet jamal | Camel meat | لحمة جمل |
| Lahmet ghanam | Goat meat | لحمة غنم |
| Jaj | chicken | جاج |
| Deek roomi | turkey | ديك رومي |
| Samak | fish | سمك |
| Akil bahri | seafood | اكل بحري |
| Gambari | shrimps | جمبري |
| Saratan | crabs | سرطان |
| Jarad el bahr | lobster | جراد البحر |
| Habbar | calamari | حبار |

# VEGETABLES

| Pronunciation | English meaning | Arabic script |
|---|---|---|
| Khodrawat | vegetables | خضروات |
| Bandoora | tomato | بندورة |
| Fifil helweh | Parika, sweet pepper | فلفل حلو |
| Filfil harr | Hot pepper | فلفل حار |
| Kheiar | cucumber | خيار |
| Jazar | carrot | جزر |
| Fejel | radish | فجل |
| Batata | potato | بطاطا |
| Batata helweh | Sweet potato | بطاطا حلوة |
| Basal | onion | بصل |
| Thawm | garlic | ثوم |
| Koosa | zukkini | كوسة |
| Baitenjaan | eggplant | بيتنجان |

| Pronunciation | English meaning | Arabic script |
|---|---|---|
| Zahra | cauliflower | زهرة |
| Shamandar | beetroot | شمندر |
| Guttain | pumpkin | قطين |
| Bamyeh | ocra | بامية |
| Sabanekh | spinach | سبانخ |
| Fool | beans | فول |
| 'Adas | lentils | عدس |
| Hommos | chickpeas | حمص |
| Bazella | Green peas | بازيلا |
| Fitir | mushrooms | فطر |
| Bagdonis | parsley | بقدونس |
| Korfos | celery | كرفس |
| Bagdonis | dill | بقدونس |
| Kozbara | coriander | كزبرة |

Notes:

## FRUITS

| Pronunciation | English meaning | Arabic script |
|---|---|---|
| Fawakeh | fruit | فواكة |
| Toffah | apple | تفاح |
| Injas | pear | انجاص |
| Mawz | banana | موز |
| Bortuqal | orange | برتقال |
| Laimoon | lemon | ليمون |
| Balah | dates | بلح |
| Teen | figs | تين |
| Shommam | melon | شمام |
| Battekh | watermelon | بطيخ |
| Khawkh | peach | خوخ |
| Mishmish | apricot | مشمش |
| Toot | blackberry, raspberry | توت |

| Pronunciation | English meaning | Arabic script |
|---|---|---|
| Farawlah | strawberry | فراولة |
| Manga | mango | مانجا |
| Jawwafa | guava | جوافة |
| Afokado | avocado | افوكادو |
| 'Enab | grapes | عنب |
| Bargoog ( khawkh ) | plum | ( برقوق ( خوخ |
| Jawz | walnuts | جوز |
| Lawz | almonds | لوز |
| Kashoo | cashew | كاشو |
| Snobar | Pine seeds | صنوبر |
| Bondog | hazelnuts | بندق |
| Fool sodani | peanuts | فول سوداني |
| Ananas | pineapple | أناناس |

**Notes:**

## SWEETS

Jordanians have a sweet tooth. Their favorite pastries would fill a whole book (coming up next, maybe) so here are just some general expressions.

| Pronunciation | English meaning | Arabic script |
|---------------|-----------------|---------------|
| Halaweiat | sweets | حلويات |
| Shokolata | chocolate | شوكولاتة |
| Helw | candy | حلو |
| Massasah | lollipop | مصاصة |
| 'Elkeh | Chewing gum | علكة |
| Baskawt | bisquits | بسكوت |
| Shebs | chips | شيبس |

Notes:

## DRINKS

Jordan is hot most of the year, you need to drink a lot of water to keep yourself hydrated.

A great variety of fruit juices, carbonated soft drinks and bottled water are sold in every shop.

Alcohol is also available in Jordan but only at licenced liquor shops, some tourist restaurants, pub and bars in bigger cities and 4-5 star hotels.

| Pronunciation | English meaning | Arabic script |
|---|---|---|
| Mashrobat | drink | المشروبات |
| Mai | water | مي |
| Haleeb | milk | حليب |
| Laban | Drink yoghurt | لبن |
| shaneeneh | Salty drink yoghurt | شنينة |
| Gahweh sada | Coffee (Arabic or Turkish) | قهوة سادة |
| Niskafeh | Coffee (Nescafe) | نسكافيه |

| Pronunciation | English meaning | Arabic script |
|---|---|---|
| Kola | coke | كولا |
| Bibsi | Pepsi | بيبسي |
| 'Aseer | juice | عصير |
| Beerah | beer | بيرة |
| Sharab Sh'eer | alcohol free beer | شراب شعير |
| Nbeed | wine | نبيذ |
| Shai | tea | شاي |
| Shai aswad | Black tea | شاي اسود |
| Shai bna'na' | Mint tea | شاي بنعنع |
| Shai akhdar | Green tea | شاي اخضر |
| Karkadeh | Hibiscus tea | كركدي |
| Thalj | Ice | ثلج |

Notes:

## SPICES & FLAVOURS

This sub-chapter could be also very long if we listed all the spices available in Jordan - but these few expressions should be enough for everyday discussions about taste of the food.

| Pronunciation | English meaning | Arabic script |
|---|---|---|
| Maleh | salty | مالح |
| Filfil | pepper | فلفل |
| Shattah | Hot (spicy) | شطة |
| Sukkar | sugar | سكر |
| Helw | sweet | حلو |
| Morr | bitter | مر |
| Hamedd | sour | حامض |
| Dafi | Hot (warm) | دافي |
| Barid | cold | بارد |

**Notes:**

# 12 SHOPPING

Haggling is common in Jordan but not as extreme as in some other Arabic countries.

You can always ask "*Is this the last price?*" but don't hope to get a good deal by offering a ridiculously low price for something.

Usually, you can try to bargain at small shops for clothes or shoes and handicrafts, at the fruits and vegetables markets, smaller hotels but
don't bargain at pharmacies, supermarkets and big stores where prices are fixed.

| Pronunciation | English meaning | Arabic script |
|---|---|---|
| *qaddaysh ha' hadda?* | How much is it? | قديش حق هاد؟ |
| *hadda gali ktiir* | That's too expensive. | غالي كتير |
| Ta'milly khasem? | Can I get a discount? | تعملي خصم ؟ |
| Ptiqbal Dollar / Euro? | Do you accept American dollars / Euro? | بتقبل دولار / يورو ؟ |
| 'Indak Visa? | Do you accept credit cards? | عندك فيزا؟ |
| 'Indak Hajem Thani? | Do you have another size? | عندك حجم ثاني؟ |
| 'Indak lawn Thani? | Do you have another color? | عندك لون ثاني؟ |
| Rkhees | Cheap | رخيص |

Notes:

# 13 FAMILY

Most Jordanian families are extended and large. Jordanians generally identify themselves according to family kinship, as well as tribal affiliation.

A Jordanian person's name consists of

1. His/her own first name

2. The father's first name

3. The grandfather's first name

4. Family (Tribe) name

## CHILDREN

The bonds in the Jordanian family are very strong. Parents watch over and are involved in every aspect of their children's lives even after they get married - unless they live far away with their new family.

Children show large amount of respect for parents especially the father. Children are also considered to be a sign of wealth and prosperity.

It is common in Jordan to call parents as the *"father and mother of X"* where the *"X"* represents their eldest son (or the eldest daughter, if there are no sons yet).

e.g. *"Abu Ahmed"* is Ahmed's father, to a man whose eldest son is called Ahmed.

His wife would be called *"Umm Ahmed"*, Ahmed's mother.

## RESPECT FOR ELDERS

Traditionally, the eldest male is undisputed head of the extended family and no undertaking could be begun without his approval.

Elders are also considered integral family members and sources of wisdom and spirituality. In everyday life respect toward elders is easily noticed.

In fact, the word of any older person is usually unquestionably followed or at least not publicly questioned.

| Pronunciation | English meaning | Arabic script |
|---|---|---|
| 'Aa'ileh | Family | عائلة |
| 'Abb | Father | أب |
| 'Omm | Mother | أم |
| 'Ibn | Son | إبن |
| Bent | Daughter | بنت |
| 'Akh | Brother | أخ |
| 'Okht | Sister | أخت |
| Jiddeh | Grandmother | جدة |
| Jidd | Grandfather | جد |
| 'Amm | Uncle (on the father's side) | عم |
| 'Ammeh | Aunt (on the father's side) | عمة |
| Khal | Uncle (on the mother's side) | خال |

| Pronunciation | English meaning | Arabic script |
|---------------|-----------------|---------------|
| Khaleh | Aunt (on the mother's side) | خالة |
| Hamat | Mother-in-law | حماة |
| Hamay | Father-in-law | حماي |
| Silf | Brother-in-law | سلف |
| Sifleh | Sister-in-law | سلفة |
| Ibn 'Amm | Cousin (male) | ابن العم |
| Bent 'Amm | Cousin (female) | بنت العم |
| Bent el 'Akh | Niece | بنت الأخ |
| 'Ibn el 'Akh | Nephew | ابن الأخ |
| Khateeb | Fiancee (male) | خطيب |
| Khateebeh | Fiancee (female) | خطيبة |
| Sadeeq | Friend (male) | صديق |
| Sadeeqah | Girlfriend (female friend) | صديقة |

**Notes:**

# 14  TRANSPORTATION

Buses, taxis and service taxis (a shared taxi) are the public transportation available in Jordan.

Buses are the most used public transportation. Men and women do not sit next to each other unless they're related.

Old people are given seats immediately as a way of showing respect.

In taxis, women should not sit in the front seat. They are also advised to avoid long eye contact and smiling at the driver.

Regular taxis are green in Aqaba and yellow in other cities of Jordan.

The *"service"* is a white taxi that can accommodate up to 5-6 passengers and the direction of it is already identified. They usually run between two cities of Jordan.

In Aqaba there are also service taxis running to certain cities in Saudi Arabia.

The regular taxis have meters so there shouldn't be any arguments about the fare. However, if you go on a longer ride, outside the city you should always discuss the price with the driver before you depart.

The table below includes "train" too, but in currently there is no train transportation in Jordan, so you can skip that.

| Pronunciation | English meaning | Arabic script |
|---|---|---|
| Bass | Bus | باص |
| Taxi | Taxi | تكسي |
| Sarvees | Service taxi | سرفيس |
| Qitar | Train | قطار |
| Mojamma' basat | Bus station | مجمع باصات |
| Mahattet qitar | Train station | محطة قطار |
| Tayyarah | Airplane | طيارة |
| Matar | Airport | مطا |
| Pronunciation | English | Arabic script |

| | meaning | |
|---|---|---|
| 'abbarah | Ferry | عبارة |
| Mahattet 'Abbarat | Ferry station / port | محطة عبارات |
| Noqtet hodood | Border station | نقطة حدود |
| Wain biroh had el bas ? | Where does this bus go? | وين بروح الباص هاد؟ |
| Wain bas el batra? | Where is the bus for Petra? | وين باص البترا؟ |
| Mata tale' bas el batra | When does the bus for Petra leave? | متى طالع باص البترا؟ |
| Mata bewsal bas el batra | When will this train/bus arrive in Petra? | متى بيوصل باص البترا؟ |
| Kam se'r el tazkirah lal batra | How much is a ticket to Petra? | كم سعر التذكرة للبترا؟ |
| Bidde tazkirah lal batra law samaht | One ticket to Petra, please. | بدي تذكرة للبترا لو سمحت |

Notes:

# 15  DIRECTIONS & FINDING YOUR WAY

Useful expressions for finding your way and get orientation.

| Pronunciation | English meaning | Arabic script |
|---|---|---|
| Wain... | Where is... | وين ... |
| Btigdar tfarjeeni 'Al Khareeta? | Can you show me on the map? | بتقدر تفرجيني عالخريطة؟ |
| Wasat el balad | Downtown | وسط البلد |
| Share' | Street | شارع |
| 'Al Yameen | To the right | عاليمين |

| Pronunciation | English meaning | Arabic script |
|---|---|---|
| 'Al Yasar | To the left | عاليسار |
| Doghri | Straight ahead | دغري |
| Ba'd el ... | After the... | بعد ال ... |
| Gabl el ... | Before the... | قبل ال ... |
| Janb el ... | Next to... | جنب ال ... |
| Gbal el ... | In front of ... | قبال ال ... |
| Wara el ... | Behind ... | ورا ... |
| Tal'a | Uphill | طلعة |
| Nazleh | Downhill | نزلة |
| Shamal | North | شمال |
| Janoub | South | جنوب |
| Sharq | East | شرق |
| Gharb | West | غرب |

Notes:

# 16 POST OFFICE, BANK & MONEY EXCHANGE

Exchange offices in Jordan buy and sell the following currencies:

USD, EUR, GBP, CHF, CAD, AUD, JPY, Egyptian Pound and the currencies of the Arab Gulf countries.

Some exchange offices also exchange NIS (New Israeli Shekel) but not all of them. Keep that in mind if you are arriving from Israel.

| Pronunciation | English meaning | Arabic script |
|---|---|---|
| Bareed | Post Office | بريد |
| Gaddesh el Bareed la Amrekia / Orobba | How much is the postage to the US /Europe? | قديش البريد لأمريكيا / أوروبا؟ |
| Bitaqa Bareediyeh | Postcard | بطاقة بريدية |
| Risaleh | Letter | رسالة |
| Tabe' | Stamp | طابع |
| Tard | Parcel | طرد |
| Bank | Bank | بنك |
| Srafeh | Money Exchange | صرافة |
| Sarraf | ATM | صراف |
| Gaddesh se'r el sarf? | What is the exchange rate? | قديش سعر الصرف؟ |

Notes:

# 17  HEALTH ISSUES

Doctors and pharmacists in Jordan get educated in English – many of them had studied abroad too – so you can discuss your problem with them in English.

However, you might find the following vocabulary useful when talking to everyday people.

| Pronunciation | English meaning | Arabic script |
|---|---|---|
| *ana mariiD* | I'm sick. | انا مريض |
| *biddi doktor* | I need a doctor. | بدي دكتور |
| Biddi doktoe asnaan | I need a dentist | بدي دكتور اسنان |
| Pronunciation | English | Arabic script |

|  | meaning |  |
|---|---|---|
| Saidaliyah | Pharmacy | صيدلية |
| Endi hararah | I have fever | عندي حرارة |
| Endi soda' | I have headcahe | عندي صداع |
| Endi maghs | I have stomach ache | عندي مغص |
| Endi isshaal | I have diarrhea | عندي اسهال |
| Dayekh | I feel dizzy | دايخ |
| Majrooh | I'm injured | مجروح |
| Banzef | I'm bleeding | بنزف |
| Law samaht itlob is'aaf | Please call an ambulance | لو سمحت اطلب الاسعاف |

Notes:

# 18 EMERGENCY SITUATIONS

Hopefully you will never need to use these words, but just in case...

Notes:

| Pronunciation | English meaning | Arabic script |
|---|---|---|
| Shourta | Police | شرطة |
| Al Shourta al Seiahiyyah | Tourist Police | الشرطة السياحية |
| Insaraget | I was robbed. | انسرقت |
| Insargat kamerti | I got my camera stolen | انسرقت كاميرتي |
| Dayya'et jawazi | I lost my passport | ضيعت جوازي |
| Had el zalameh bidayegni | This man is harrassing me. | هاد الزلمة بذايقني |
| Sa'dooni! | Help! | إساعدوني |
| Ib'ed 'Anni! | Leave me alone! | إبعد عني! |
| Rah Atlob el Shourta | I will call the police. | راح اطلب الشرطة |

# EMERGENCY PHONE NUMBERS IN JORDAN

**911** Jordan's centralized emergency line.

Call this number if you need immediate police or medical assistance.

## Additional emergency numbers

**196** Public Security Directorate

**199** Civil Defense (Paramedics, Fire Fighters)

**190** Traffic Police

**191** Rescue Police

**192** Metropolitan Police

**194** Highway Patrols

## TOURIST POLICE IN JORDAN

You can find Tourism Police huts at all major tourist attractions in Jordan and the best way to contact them is by person.

The Tourism Police belongs to the Public Security Directorate (PSD) and it is supposed to have a website: http://www.tourist-police.psd.gov.jo/en/

BUT, at the time of writing, it doesn't work.

The PSD website itself is only in Arabic, doesn't seem to have an English version.. http://www.psd.gov.jo/index.php

However, they do have an email address, where you can write in English:

tourist.dept@psd.gov.jo

You may also try to call their central number by dialing **196** first and then extention **4661** or by one of the numbers below:

| Petra Tourism Police | +962 3 215 6441 |
|---|---|
| Wadi Rum Tourism Police | +962 3 209 0600<br>+962 3 201 8215 |
| Aqaba Tourism Police (Police Station) | +962 3 203 4118 |

## FOREIGN EMBASSIES IN JORDAN

You can find the contact details of foreign embassies and consulates in Jordan on the Jordan eGoverment website. Direct link:

http://www.jordan.gov.jo/wps/portal/!
ut/p/b1/04_SjzQyMDA3MDA1sLDQj9CPykssy0xPL
MnMz0vMAfGjzOLDLL0twrzdDQ0sPNwtDDy9DIz
MfM2djA3CDPWDU_P0c6McFQFXn8xi/

If you are reading this book as an digital document, you can just simply click on it.

However, if you are actually holding a paper book in your hand, then type this into your web browser:

http://www.jordan.gov.jo

Choose English at the bottom left corner and then click the *"Visitors"* tab on the menu.

Then click the *"Foreign Diplomatic Missions in Jordan" link under "Related Information".*

Your embassy contact details:

And here is the last vocabulary table of this book:

| Pronunciation | English meaning | Arabic script |
| --- | --- | --- |
| Jawaz safar | Passport | جواز السفر |
| Visa | Visa | فيزا |
| Safarah | Embassy | سفارة |
| Qonsoliyeh | Consulate | قنصلية |

# 19  JORDAN TRAVEL RESOURCES

## www.Go2Jordan.INFO

This is an ongoing project of mine, a website that I started in 2008.

My goal is to collect and share all kind of Jordan-related information that is useful for travelers and expats.

Apart from information provided by Jordanian tourism official sources I also publish first-hand travelers' experiences, tips and hints.

Facebook: https://www.facebook.com/Go2Jordan

Twitter: https://twitter.com/EsTeh

## VisitJordan.com

The official website of the **Jordan Tourism Board**.

## HotelsCombined

https://www.hotelscombined.com/Place/Jordan.htm?a_aid=7264&label=tsaj

The most popular online hotel price comparison site lists a wide variety of accommodation options in Jordan.

Not only hotels in all price ranges but also hostels, guest houses, B-and-Bs, furnished apartments and Bedouin desert camps too.

The booking process is easy and streamlined, and no booking fees or deposits to be paid.

Tripadvisor Jordan Forums

Probably the best online travel forum with very active and helpful members who will be happy to share their knowledge and experiences with you.

# 20 ARABIC LANGUAGE RESOURCES

## Learning Arabic in Jordan

Want to learn Arabic in Jordan?

Here are just a few links to various language schools offering Arabic courses to foreigners in Jordan:

## Amman

Kelsey Arabic Program

The Kelsey Arabic Program is an Arabic language program located in Amman, Jordan. Their students come from around the world to learn Arabic. They have facilities in Amman, Madaba and Mafraq.

## University of Jordan's Language Center

Since its inception in 1979, the University of Jordan Language Center (UJLC) has been offering courses in modern standard Arabic of various levels. Presently, LC offers six levels of intensive study: Arabic for beginners, remedial, pre-intermediate, intermediate, upper intermediate, and advanced. All six levels are offered regularly and concurrently during the fall, spring, and summer semesters. Registration in the advanced level is dependent upon the enrollment of a sufficient number of students. The emphasis in the program is on modern standard Arabic. Other levels are offered upon request.

## Qasid Arabic Institute

Apart from Modern Standard Arabic, they also offer courses in Classical Arabic and Colloquial (Ammiya) Arabic.

Qasid students have come as young as 15 and as old as 65, including consulate officers, Fulbright researchers, full-time mothers, medical doctors, FLAS recipients, and Ivy League graduates, and hail from nearly two dozen countries.

## Aqaba

### LIFE Center

The **Life Center** has regular Arabic language courses for foreigners. Located on the central street of the area called "Mahdood".

Note: on the Aqaba map you will find it as "Hay Ar Rawda", this is the official name of this neighborhood but everybody in Aqaba calls it "Mahdood".

## Learn Arabic Online

If you are interested in gaining a more in-depth knowledge of Arabic and want to learn at your own pace, I recommend you to check out these online resources:

### Arabic Language FAQ

This page is a great resource put together by a student who's been studying Arabic since 2005.

### Learn Koran Online

If you want to read the Holy Koran you will need to learn classical Arabic. This is one of the many websites out there that teaches the Koran for English speakers.

<u>Rocket Arabic</u>

After carefully reviewing quite a few online Arabic courses, Arabic language softwares as well as Arabic language books on the internet, I picked **Rocket Arabic**, which is the **best value-for-money** Arabic language course available online.

It focuses on the Egyptian Arabic dialect, which is the most widely spoken and understood in all over the Arab world, thanks to the dominance of Egyptian music and films in the popular culture.

This course has been around for several years now and proved to be very popular among Arabic learners. In 2011 it got updated with **brand new learning tools** to help you stay motivated and get the most out of your learning time.

The lessons are downloadable, so you can take them with you anywhere and do not need to be online all the time if you want to study or practise.

**What is included in the Rocket Arabic online course:**

**31 Interactive Audio Lessons** with modern, everyday Arabic conversations that you can take part in. These tracks average 20 minutes in length - that's over 13 hours of audio lessons. (Downloadable)

**7 practical topics** that include greetings, meetings,

food and drink, travel, in town, arts and culture, family and friends, and tradition.

**31 Arabic Language Lessons**, with step-by-step explanations, over 900 embedded audio clips with examples, and instant feedback quizzes, to help you speak Arabic naturally.

**31 Arabic Writing Lessons**, with easy to follow videos and explanations, so you can learn to read and write Arabic.

**31 Arabic Culture Lessons** that give you insights into a wide variety of situations you're likely to encounter in Arabic speaking countries, so you can get the most out of your experience.

**MegaArabic Software Games** to increase the number of Arabic words you know, improve your understanding of spoken Arabic, and help you master Arabic characters. (Downloadable)

Full access to the **Rocket Arabic Motivation Center** where you'll learn tried and tested techniques that can reduce your learning time by up to 50%!

**My Vocab** is an interactive online tool that helps you learn and remember the words in your own Arabic vocabulary list.

**Progress Tracking** so you always know which Rocket Arabic lessons, quizzes and tests you've completed, and where you're headed next on our recommended learning path.

**Instant Feedback Quizzes and Self-Tests** so you can see how much your Arabic has improved!

**Rocket Arabic Premium Certification** to boost your Arabic speaking confidence!

**Personal Support** - the Rocket Arabic teachers will be with you every step of the way. You'll have full access to the Rocket Arabic **Learner's Forum**, where you'll have all your Arabic language questions answered!

**Lifetime membership**, so you can take your time, and refer back to your course for as long as you need.

**24/7 online access** to all your course materials so you can learn Arabic anywhere, anytime.

**Downloadable lessons and games** so you don't always have to be online.

**MP3/iPod compatible audio** so you can learn on the move or anywhere you need to be.

**Mac/PC compatible lessons** so you can use the

course        on        any        computer.

**Technical Support** - The Rocket Languages technical support team is just an email or phone call    away    if    you    need    them.

**Free Rocket Arabic Premium online upgrades** so you can feel confident that you're always learning with the most up to date Arabic course on the market, in the easiest possible way.

>> Click here to check out their FREE trial from the official website <<

# 21 GET THIS BOOK IN OTHER FORMATS

This book is also available in the following formats:

**Kindle**

http://www.amazon.com/gp/product/B00D3J2Y4K

Actually, the Kindle version was published before the paperback, back in 2012.

Please be aware that Kindle is currently not supporting Arabic script so I had to convert the vocabulary tables into images.

It means that while the body text of the book can be enlarged on your Kindle reader, the images with the Arabic script have a fixed size.

**PDF download**

https://gumroad.com/l/JordanianArabic

# ABOUT THE AUTHOR

Eszter Papai, born in Hungary, has been living in Aqaba (Jordan) since 2005.

Her website (www.Go2Jordan.INFO - Your Guide to Aqaba and Jordan), visited daily by hundreds of travelers, is a great resource of insider travel information about Jordan.

Made in the USA
Las Vegas, NV
14 March 2022